THE WESTERN AROUND LONDON
A Colour Portfolio

Ian Allan
PUBLISHING

Kevin McCormack

Previous Page: One of only four 'Castles' to last beyond February 1965, No 7034 *Ince Castle* is seen on 8 September 1962. The location is Purley-on-Thames, west of Tilehurst, which had a wonderful 'shanty town' between the railway and the river (although the local council was less impressed!). The site's ramshackle buildings included various old buses and railway carriages converted into homes, including three GWR Third-class family saloons. Purley's best 'des res' is featured on page 37. *Derek Penney*

Above: Although the Radley–Abingdon branch was closed to passengers from 9 September 1963, freight services continued into the 1980s, due mainly to the MG car factory being located at Abingdon. Showing no evidence of the cleanliness it obtained from railtour duty in the summer, '57xx' pannier tank No 9773 shunts wagons at Abingdon station in October 1965. The last engines to visit Abingdon in steam were Nos 1466 and 6106, on 23 May 1970 for the town's carnival. However, due to the steam ban, they were not allowed to operate the line, a DMU having to be used instead. *Vernon Murphy*

Introduction

The Western around London is a companion volume to my previous railway title, *The Southern around London*, published by Ian Allan in 2003.

I spent virtually the whole of my first 25 years living in Ealing, West London, and shopping trips to The Broadway as a small boy were only bearable if my mother took me to a bench on Haven Green overlooking the main line from Paddington to the West. When I discovered the Ian Allan spotting books and was allowed to roam on my bicycle, I watched the trains at West Ealing, either from the milk bay or from Jacob's Ladder (the footbridge west of the station).

In the latter years of the 1950s steam still reigned supreme, and the locomotives hauling the expresses to and from London, usually 'Kings' and 'Castles', weren't just clean — they positively sparkled. Representatives from all the Great Western 4-6-0 classes used to appear, including the last 'Stars', although 'Manors' were very rare. We also had our own classes not normally found elsewhere on the Western Region — the 'condensing' pannier tanks, designed to travel on London Transport (LT) tracks, and the '61xx' large Prairie tanks, nicknamed 'tanner-oners', which monopolised the suburban workings. Then we had our push-and-pulls (auto-trains) and long-distance freight trains (which we hoped would not be hauled by clanking 'WDs')

First published 2004

ISBN 0 7110 3027 8

Published by Ian Allan Publishing

an imprint of Ian Allan Publishing Ltd, Hersham, Surrey KT12 4RG.
Printed by Ian Allan Printing Ltd, Hersham, Surrey KT12 4RG.

Code: 0409/B2

and that wretched diesel parcels van, W34W, which never seemed to be far away.

Sometimes a fantastic 'cop' would come along. My rarest sightings were of ROD 2-8-0 No 3031 passing through Castle Bar Park Halt on the Greenford loop and 2-8-2 tank No 7202 (now preserved at Didcot) trundling through West Ealing, both hauling goods trains. But where was that elusive 'Castle', No 5050 *Earl of St Germans*?

Towards the end of the 1950s the main-line diesels began to arrive. But Great Western Railway (GWR) traditions clung on, and the 'Kings' and 'Castles' working alongside the first diesels were still kept generally presentable — at least up to the end of 1962, and in some cases into 1963 (although the 'Kings' had been withdrawn by then). However, by the summer of 1964, when the last steam-hauled express trains, on the Paddington–Worcester services, had been 'dieselised', the external condition of the surviving steam engines deteriorated rapidly. It seemed that things couldn't get any worse, but they did. The start of 1965 — the last year of Western Region (WR) steam — saw the remaining 4-6-0s lose their nameplates, and most locomotives had their numberplates removed as well. By this time the only scheduled steam-hauled passenger train out of Paddington was the 4.15pm to Banbury, and that ceased on 11 June. With the exception of No 7029 *Clun Castle*, which sometimes worked this service (albeit not always with its plates attached), the motive power for this train looked in a disgusting state. Indeed, *Clun Castle* and large Prairie No 6106 were the only presentable steam engines to be found on normal workings in the London area, and that was only because they had 'friends' who were trying to save them (successfully, thank goodness).

It was very distressing for GWR enthusiasts to see the old company's beautiful locomotives, with their brass and copper and lined-green livery, deteriorate so rapidly and then for the WR to be the first Region to eradicate steam. Luckily, the activities of the preservationists brought some comfort when Western steam officially ended on 31 December 1965 — particularly, as far as the London area was concerned, the rising Great Western Society (GWS). Through the good offices of WR management, the GWS was able to keep preserved locomotives and rolling stock at Taplow goods shed and subsequently at Didcot engine shed, as well as make occasional steam forays onto British Railways (BR) lines. The latter activities ceased in September 1968 due to the nationwide steam ban, but just over three years later the ban was lifted, and the rest is history.

My earlier book on the London area, *Glory Days: Western Region Steam around London*, published by Ian Allan in 1998, covered lines as far as Maidenhead and High Wycombe. Now the boundaries are extended to show workings in the 1950s and 1960s mainly within an arc running roughly north from Reading up to Oxford and then across to Aylesbury (then a London Transport Underground and Country Bus outpost). There is also some coverage of ex-GWR locomotives working close to London on other BR Regions and LT.

My own colour transparencies have been augmented by the photographs of several contributors whose assistance has been vital, and my sincere thanks go to David Clark (for his material and that of the late Ken Wightman), Jim Oatway, Geoff Rixon, Roy Hobbs, Derek Penney, Marcus Eavis, Vernon Murphy, Charles Firminger, Bill Piggott, Nick Lera, Neil Davenport, Frank Dumbleton and Bruce Jenkins.

We are very lucky to have such a large collection of Great Western locomotives preserved today — a situation completely unforeseen at the end of 1965, when it seemed that just a few would be saved. For this change of fortune we must, of course, be eternally grateful to the late Dai Woodham, of Barry scrapyard fame, and to the continuing (and hopefully not dwindling) band of enthusiasts who give up their time to restore these wonderful machines and keep them running. Also, we must not forget the historic rolling stock and other artefacts which help keep the GWR's memory alive today.

Amazingly, the Barry legacy has not yet ended, due to the survival of the so-called 'Barry Ten' surplus locomotives. 'Hall' No 4942 left long ago to become a donor engine for a new Churchward 'Saint' being built by the GWS, which has also announced that it hopes to build a Hawksworth 'County' from the frames of 'Hall' No 7927 and the boiler of Stanier '8F' No 48518. Other parts from Nos 4942 and 7927 could also help create a new 'Grange' (another missing GWR type), which a group based on the Llangollen Railway is planning to build. Further possibilities include a Churchward 'County' 4-4-2 tank, based on 2-6-2 tank No 4115, and a '47xx' 2-8-0. The 'Barry Ten' will thus provide an opportunity to put the GWR's standardisation policy into action in the 21st century!

Kevin R. McCormack
Ashtead, Surrey
March 2004

3

No 5015 *Kingswear Castle* stands in Brunel's magnificent cathedral at Paddington after bringing the 4.25pm from Fishguard into Platform 8 on 18 August 1962. Paddington station was completed in 1854 and is, of course, still fulfilling the role for which it was designed. *Geoff Rixon*

Travelling from Paddington on the Bristol and Oxford line, the first opportunity for engines to quench their thirst while on the move was at Goring troughs, between Reading and Didcot. Scooping up water in this view is No 5007 *Rougemont Castle*, hauling a milk train. This locomotive entered service in June 1927 and was withdrawn in September 1962. *Ken Wightman*

The largest class of GWR-designed 4-6-0s were the 'Halls', which numbered 330. These mixed-traffic locomotives, designed by Collett and (in 'Modified' form) Hawksworth, represented a smaller-wheeled development of Churchward's 'Saint' passenger locomotives. No 4929 *Goytrey Hall*, one of the earlier 'Halls', stands at Reading General on 24 March 1963. *Jim Oatway*

Almost a year has elapsed since No 7022 *Hereford Castle* was spruced up as a standby engine for the Ian Allan railtour of 9 May 1964, when it was hoped to match the 100mph-plus recorded by *City of Truro* exactly 60 years earlier. Apparently never cleaned since and by now devoid of nameplates and numberplates, the locomotive, one of the last four 'Castles' in service, is seen on 28 April 1965 eking out its last few weeks on the 4.15pm from Paddington to Banbury. This view was taken from Carr Road footbridge as the train, running parallel with the London Transport (LT) Central Line, approaches Northolt station. *Bill Piggott*

Left: Flat-cabbed pannier tank No 5755 from Slough shed trundles through Sonning Cutting, east of Reading, with an up freight in August 1958. This engine narrowly missed having a second career with LT, Nos 5752, 5757 and 5764 (amongst others) getting the call. *Ken Wightman*

Above: Immaculately turned-out 4-6-0 No 4089 *Donnington Castle* simmers at Old Oak Common shed on 15 April 1961. The locomotive was completed in July 1925 and would have run originally with a 3,500-gallon low-sided tender. The higher 4,000-gallon tender with which the 'Castles' were later paired was introduced in 1926, but, like many of the class in later years, No 4089 has a straight-sided Hawksworth tender. *Jim Oatway*

Above: Although this shot at Banbury is somewhat out of range for this book, the train will come into the area of coverage when it reaches its final destination at Princes Risborough. Besides, it's a rather rare colour view from 1958 depicting a member of the pannier-tank class with the largest wheels — auto-fitted No 5407. The locomotive ended up at Woodham's scrapyard in 1960 but was too early to escape scrapping. *Marcus Eavis*

Right: Also heading for Princes Risborough in 1958 but from a different direction is large Prairie tank No 6117, hauling a standard suburban five-coach set. The train has just left the former Great Central/LT line at Aylesbury, and some brown Metropolitan carriages can be seen in the background. LT retreated from Aylesbury to Amersham in September 1961, when steam working from Rickmansworth was discontinued. *Marcus Eavis*

Left: The pride of the Western for 35 years was the pioneer 'King' locomotive, No 6000 *King George V*, which in 1927 travelled to the USA, where it gained the buffer-beam bell and the medals on the cab side. 'KG5', as it is colloquially known, became a pioneer again in October 1971, when, through the amazing efforts of H. P. Bulmer Ltd, it hauled a promotional train over four days, which led directly to the lifting of the steam ban on BR. This famous machine is seen at Old Oak Common shed on 15 April 1961. *Jim Oatway*

Above: Another view of the last scheduled steam-hauled passenger service from Paddington — the 4.15pm to Banbury — in its last few weeks of operation, in May 1965. Motive power is No 6829 *Burmington Grange*, and the location is between Hanger Lane and the site of Brentham Halt. In the background to the left is the Virol factory, home of that brown stodge that Mother made you eat to help build you up! *Author*

Left: Sonning Cutting was an attractive setting for steam photography, but the amount of summer foliage meant that, for best results in colour, trains normally had to be entering or leaving the cutting even when there was a high sun. Shadows are lengthening as No 5999 *Wollaton Hall* heads towards Twyford with a rake of prewar Collett coaches in August 1958. *Ken Wightman*

Above: The last regular passenger services to be hauled by Western steam engines in the Thames Valley were the cross-Region trains travelling via Oxford from the North and Midlands to the South Coast. One such train, headed by an unidentified 'Grange' 4-6-0, is seen crossing Gatehampton bridge, near Goring & Streatley, in September 1965. This was an unplanned photograph taken from a boat cruising along the River Thames. *Vernon Murphy*

Churchward's nine massive '47xx' 2-8-0s are sadly missed by enthusiasts today, but there is talk of constructing a new one. Here Southall-based No 4707 visits Old Oak Common, where several were shedded, on 16 August 1959. The locomotive looks in fine fettle, considering it was involved in a serious derailment near Swindon the previous November. *Ken Wightman*

Tyseley-based Churchward Mogul No 5369 takes on water at Guildford while working a Birmingham–Eastbourne train in 1959. The locomotive would not be allowed beyond Redhill. *Marcus Eavis*

Above: The unsung heroes of the Western must have been Churchward's '28xx' class of freight locomotives. The prototype, constructed in 1903, was the first 2-8-0 in Britain, and the 83 engines which followed were built between 1905 and 1919. No 2841, seen here in August 1958 near Twyford, was completed in 1912 and gave 51 years' service.
Ken Wightman

Right: Once referred to in a TV script as 'Bert & Agnes Hall', following filming at Didcot Railway Centre in 1971, but in reality named after a stately home near Bridlington in Yorkshire, No 6998 looks every bit a GWR thoroughbred despite having been completed by BR in 1949. This view shows the locomotive at Southall shed on 12 April 1963.
Jim Oatway

Left: The engine that gave rise to the 'Royal Scot' class! In 1926 No 5000 *Launceston Castle* was borrowed by the LMS for testing on the West Coast main line while the company was trying to find a suitable express passenger type, even contemplating placing an order with the GWR for 'Castle' locomotives. Not surprisingly, the engine performed very well, as another 'Castle' (No 4079) had done the previous year on the LNER during the 1925 Locomotive Exchanges. Here, No 5000 is seen preparing to depart from Paddington on 18 August 1962. *Geoff Rixon*

Below: What a bore these local trains were to 1950s trainspotters waiting for an exciting 'cop'; the 'tanner-oner' would be greeted with cries of 'scrap it'! Little did we know how soon this would happen, although some of these stalwarts survived the DMU onslaught and lasted until the end of 1965 on miscellaneous duties. This view, dating from 6 October 1958, depicts No 6136 approaching Hanwell & Elthorne station. *Ken Wightman*

Below: Although favoured by LT for their reduced height, the flat-cabbed pannier tanks were older than the higher-cabbed versions, and the London sheds got rid of them before the later ones, apart from No 8743. This scene shows the locomotive on one of the turntable roads inside Old Oak Common shed in April 1964. *Author*

Right: Inter-regional trains were a feature of the GWR line between Reading and Oxford, regularly bringing Southern locomotives to Oxford and Western ones to Basingstoke. On 27 June 1959 No 6929 *Whorlton Hall*, still carrying the early-style lion-and-wheel emblem, prepares to leave Basingstoke for Banbury. *Jim Oatway*

23

Left: During a visit to Reading on 2 January 1965, the last official day of steam working on the Southern's Reading–Redhill line (which included a working by No 7829 *Ramsbury Manor*), No 6161 was captured on film at the eastern end of Reading General station. The trainspotters seem more interested in main-line activity — or maybe they are just admiring the semaphore signals! *Author*

Above: The arrival in late 1963 in the London area of five small Prairie tanks superfluous in the West Country came as a great surprise, but they slotted in well between the larger '61xx' class and the smaller pannier tanks. This view of No 5531 working hard at West Drayton was recorded in December 1964, immediately before the locomotive's withdrawal. It would be over 20 years before one of these engines again hauled a freight (albeit an unusual one) on the main line in the London area, No 5572 heading a train of preserved rolling stock between Reading and Didcot in June 1985. *Author*

Left: Fitted with a double chimney for improved performance, No 5064 *Bishop's Castle* hauls an up express near Maidenhead in September 1962. For the first three months of its existence, in 1937, this engine was named *Tretower Castle*, a name later bestowed upon No 5094. *Derek Penney*

Above: A cluster of 'Halls' congregate around the rear of Didcot shed in January 1965, No 6921 *Borwick Hall* being the locomotive sporting a red cabside numberplate. On the right is the Lifting Shop, subsequently extended by the GWS. The track in the foreground leads to the turntable, which was removed by BR and has now been replaced by a larger one from Southampton Docks. *Roy Hobbs*

Above: Southern meets Western at Oxford on 1 August 1964. Rebuilt 'West Country' No 34021 *Dartmoor* waits at signals as 'Castle' No 5054 *Earl of Ducie* departs for London. Taking its name from a 'Dukedog' 4-4-0 in 1937, this 'Castle' clocked 102mph on 1 April 1964 when on test for the intended 'ton-up' 'Castle' trip of 9 May. By the end of November it had been ignominiously broken up inside its birthplace. *Bruce Jenkins*

Right: Collett '2884' 2-8-0 No 3839 faces the wrong way in Twyford station at the head of a ballast train as engineering staff replace a section of track on the down main line. There were 83 of these heavy-freight engines built, following on from Churchward's original class of 84 locomotives. *Nick Lera*

Left: LT was not the only 'foreign' operator of GWR pannier tanks in the London area, the Southern Region using them for a time on Clapham Junction–Waterloo empty-stock workings. One such engine, No 4601, was photographed at Nine Elms shed (now the site of New Covent Garden Market) on 19 May 1961. *Jim Oatway*

Above: The 4.15 to Banbury was often hauled by one of three 'Castles' (Nos 5042, 7022 and 7029) in the last few months of steam operation, but No 7029 *Clun Castle* was specially prepared on 19 May 1965 because Peter Lemar of the GWS was travelling on the footplate. The author, who, after school swimming at Ealing baths, had seen the locomotive travelling light engine from Southall shed, raced over to Gerrards Cross on his Honda 50 to travel on the train to Beaconsfield, where this shot was taken. *Author*

Above: Collett push-and-pull locomotive No 1440, coupled to BR auto-trailer *Wren*, takes water at a 'foreign' station — Aylesbury Town, on the ex-Great Central line from Marylebone and the ex-Metropolitan Railway from Baker Street. The author recalls when the regular GW auto engine, for a long time No 1473, was shedded at Aylesbury, which was latterly a sub-shed of Neasden. The Ian Allan locoshed book gave only the main shed allocation, so the author, as a young schoolboy, once asked railwaymen at Neasden if this 0-4-2 tank was on shed and was puzzled by the total ignorance and incredulity shown! *Marcus Eavis*

Right: Although never shedded there, Western engines did however drop in to Neasden for servicing when bringing football supporters to cup finals or internationals at nearby Wembley. One such occasion was 2 May 1959, when No 7026 *Tenby Castle*, a Wolverhampton (Stafford Road) locomotive, arrived for its break. *Jim Oatway*

Although still open for freight for most of its original length, the Southall–Brentford Dock branch closed to passengers in 1942, except for the occasional special. On 25 July 1965 '57xx' pannier tank No 9773 heads a railtour under Windmill Bridge, named after the former Southall Mill but popularly known as Three Bridges. This remarkable structure serving road, canal and railway was one of Brunel's last works, having been completed for the line's opening in July 1859. *Roy Hobbs*

The Henley-on-Thames branch from Twyford still has a passenger service today, but Wargrave, one of the two intermediate stations, had already lost one track, a platform and its covered footbridge when this view was recorded on 25 July 1965. Now, virtually everything has gone, Wargrave having been reduced to an unstaffed halt. The motive power for the railtour shown here was large Prairie tank No 6106, which surprisingly had received a heavy overhaul at Swindon as late as July 1964. This was not to be its last visit to the branch, for it returned, in steam, exactly two years later in connection with Henley's town festival on 24/25 July 1967. *Roy Hobbs*

Above: Another inter-Regional working — a York–Bournemouth train comprising Southern coaching stock — arrives at Oxford behind No 6927 *Lilford Hall* in the summer of 1962. *Marcus Eavis*

Right: Dean Third-class saloon No 2511 (later No 9317) masquerading as 10 River Gardens, Purley-on-Thames, when discovered during a boating holiday in July 1969. Built at Swindon in 1894, this private-hire carriage was withdrawn in 1937, whereupon the body became a Thames-side bungalow. In 1972 it became the author's indulgence and was transported to Didcot Railway Centre, where, the following year, it was united with the six-wheeled underframe belonging to tool van No DW109. No 2511 is remarkable in having retained most of its original fittings and furnishings, thanks to ownership by a succession of elderly ladies who were not DIY-orientated! *Frank Dumbleton*

Above : The first and last steam trains on the Underground were hauled by GWR locomotives — a broad-gauge Gooch 2-4-0 in 1863 and a '57xx' 0-6-0PT in 1971. Between 1956 and 1963 LT built up a fleet of 11 pannier tanks (excluding two which were replaced), and these were used on freight duties to replace LT's aged locomotives. Most were kept at Neasden, but a few were housed at Lillie Bridge (near Earl's Court), where this view of L92 (ex-GWR No 5786, now preserved) was recorded in May 1969. Cromwell Road is in the background. *Author*

Right: Although this scene has changed over the years, the signalbox has not and is still in use. Before the arrival of the 'Manor' 4-6-0s the Western's contribution to the running of passenger services on the Southern's Reading–Redhill line during the period covered by this book was normally to provide one service a day (Mondays to Fridays) in each direction, usually hauled by a Churchward Mogul, with additional workings at weekends. No 6379 makes a storming start from Reigate in December 1961. *Roy Hobbs*

Left and below left: A contrast in GWR branch termini — a typical rural example at Wallingford and the more urban version typified by Uxbridge (Vine Street). The branch to Wallingford from Cholsey & Moulsford opened in 1866 and closed to passengers in 1959 and to freight in 1981. It is now operated by the Cholsey & Wallingford Railway Preservation Society. Unfortunately it was not possible to preserve the terminus, which was severed from the rest of the line and is now the site of a housing estate. The branch from West Drayton & Yiewsley to Uxbridge opened in 1856 and closed to passengers in 1962 and to freight in 1964. It was dismantled in 1965, locomotives Nos 6117 and 8481 being used to haul the wagons carrying the rails and sleepers. Today there is no trace of the terminus. These views date from April 1968 and November 1964 respectively. *Author*

This is not any grubby old 'Grange' locomotive but one of only three recorded as running with a Hawksworth flat-sided tender (the other two occurrences being in 1953/4). The 'Granges' were an intermediate class between the 'Halls' and the 'Manors', closer in fact to 'Halls' in appearance but distinguishable by the raised running-plate over the cylinders. No 6844 *Penhydd Grange* acquired this tender in July 1962 and was photographed at Old Oak Common in October 1963. *Author's collection*

Left: This photograph, taken at Paddington in April 1964, depicts the familiar scene of GWR pannier tanks and a red LT Metropolitan Line train. Incredibly, these two operations were to combine to produce the sight of GWR engines at Paddington beyond the end of 1965, even if it meant a visit in the early hours! For example, pannier tank No 5764 (alias LT No L95) was photographed standing in Platform 15 on the 12.30am workmen's train from Lillie Bridge on 24 May 1969. So normal workings of Western steam locomotives into Paddington did *not* cease at the end of 1965! *Author*

Above: A reminder of the time when express engines were still kept clean, before the era when the only colour visible was on a small part of the cab side where the engine crew threw out their tea dregs! One of 15 'Castles' converted from 'Star' 4-6-0s, No 5090 *Neath Abbey* started life as No 4070 in 1923 (just a few months before the first 'Castle' was built) and was converted in 1939. This is the oldest photograph in the book, dating from 23 July 1954, and shows the locomotive departing from Oxford. *Neil Davenport*

Above: On its way from Marlow, the 'Donkey' crosses the Abbotsbrook, alongside Bourne End Marina on the River Thames, on 14 April 1962, during the last few months of steam operation. Steam would return for one day only — 15 July 1973 — to commemorate the centenary of the Bourne End–Marlow branch, with No 1450 (deputising for No 1466) working an auto-train on that line and Nos 6106 and 6998 hauling Maidenhead–Bourne End trains. *Nick Lera*

Right: No 7920 *Coney Hall* has just left the West of England main line at Old Oak West Junction and taken the 4.15pm to Banbury onto the Birmingham line. This was Paddington's last scheduled steam-hauled passenger service and ran for the last time on Friday 11 June 1965, attracting national newspaper coverage. No 7920 is depicted on 12 May 1965, hauling the customary light load of four carriages and a van. *Bill Piggott*

Left: The West Drayton & Yiewsley–Staines West branch opened in 1885 and closed to passengers on 27 March 1965. Pannier tank No 9773 is seen at the terminus while working a railtour on 25 July 1965. The line, which remains open for freight as far as Colnbrook, can be seen from the M25/M4 interchange, but viewing by drivers at this spot is not recommended! The station house at Staines West pre-dates the railway and survives today as offices. *David Clark*

Above: The cleaners have done a wonderful job on this 'King', apart from the copper-capped chimney, which seems to have been forgotten. No 6012 *King Edward VI* storms towards Hanwell & Elthorne station with the down 'Merchant Venturer' to Weston-super-Mare on 6 October 1958. Three members of this class of 30 survive today — Nos 6000, 6023 and 6024. *Ken Wightman*

Below: Deep in the bowels of Old Oak Common shed, in the corner where minor repairs were carried out, stands one of Churchward's nine magnificent '47xx' 2-8-0s, No 4703. This locomotive, dating from 1922, would be withdrawn in May 1964 and already looks somewhat down-at-heel in this April 1962 view. Designed as mixed-traffic rather than freight engines, they reached the pinnacle of their long career in 1958, when they were rostered to haul Saturday workings of the 'Royal Duchy' express, looking superb in their lined-green livery with headboard on the front. *Geoff Rixon*

Right: The down 'Pembroke Coast Express', hauled by 'Castle' No 5074 *Hampden*, speeds along near Twyford on 10 September 1960. Completed in July 1938 as *Denbigh Castle*, this engine was one of 12 'Castles' to be renamed between September 1940 and January 1941 after World War 2 aircraft. Their original 'Castle' names were given to later engines; *Denbigh Castle* was carried by No 7001 and No 7032 (though not at the same time!). *Ken Wightman*

Left: Action Stations at sleepy Loudwater in September 1965, as large Prairie tank No 6156, still in black livery, hauls a freight train past a Maidenhead–High Wycombe DMU. Until 1962 the 'Marlow Donkey' worked some services along this line to High Wycombe, where it could meet up with an auto-train for Princes Risborough and Banbury or Aylesbury. The section of line between Bourne End and High Wycombe was closed in 1970, and the track lifted. *Author*

Above: Didcot MPD in 1969, when the GWS still shared the shed with BR (and with the owners of No 4079 *Pendennis Castle* — which has now returned there via Australia). Collett 0-4-2 tank No 1466 was purchased by the GWS as a runner for £750 (including spares and delivery) in early 1964 and, until moved from Totnes to Didcot, on 2 December 1967 (under its own power, with No 6998 *Burton Agnes Hall* and miscellaneous rolling stock), had spent its entire working life in the West Country. Large Prairie tank No 6106 arrived at Didcot on 4 November 1967 from the former GWS depot at Taplow (following an extraordinary stock movement earlier in the day, which involved trips to London and Oxford). *Author*

Above: New Morris Oxfords and Mini Minors from the BMC factory at Cowley travel the iron road through Purley behind large Prairie tank No 6161 in September 1962. With higher boiler pressure than the similar '41xx' and '51xx' classes, the '61xx' class of 70 locomotives was specifically designed for London suburban services. Built between 1931 and 1935, they replaced earlier classes on these duties, notably the 'County' 4-4-2 tanks, until themselves superseded by DMUs, after which they were given more menial tasks such as this. *Derek Penney*

Right: The 'Kings' were the GWR's most powerful locomotives, but their weight restricted their route availability, and they were therefore less versatile than the 'Castles', which could do most of the work of a 'King'. In this view, recorded on 25 March 1961, No 6020 *King Henry IV* rests at Old Oak Common shed after hauling an express on the Birmingham line. Unusually, the reporting number is not obscuring the smokebox numberplate. *Jim Oatway*

Above: An unusual type of pannier tank to find anywhere remotely near London was the '16xx' class, Hawksworth's updated version of the Dean '2021' design of 1897. Smaller and lighter than the standard Collett pannier tanks, the '16xx' locomotives dated from 1949 and were thus BR-built. Working on the Watlington branch in 1961, this example, No 1636, is seen shunting at Chinnor, where a cement works and a woodyard generated rail traffic. BR freight workings ceased on 20 December 1989, and the following month the Chinnor & Princes Risborough Railway Association moved in. *Author*

Right: Not Ivor the engine but Iver the place (near Slough), with 'Modified Hall' No 7903 *Foremarke Hall* running through with a train of vans on 3 March 1963. There were 330 members of the 'Hall' class, including the prototype (a converted 'Saint') and 71 'Modified Halls'. These later locomotives, starting with No 6959, were instantly recognisable from the front by the plate-framed bogie, but the main difference from a performance point of view was the fitting of a large three-row superheater. *Derek Penney*

A visit to Cheltenham Races by train in March 1964 included a convenient stop at Reading alongside No 7808 *Cookham Manor*, which was duly photographed, some two months after its return to traffic following a heavy intermediate overhaul at Swindon. Built in 1938, this locomotive was the only 'Manor' to continue running after withdrawal on 31 December 1965 (hauling a GWS railtour in September 1966) and now resides at Didcot. Another eight from this class of 30 are preserved elsewhere. *Author*

Two of Southall's small stud of '55xx' small Prairie tanks are seen in December 1963, soon after their unexpected arrival in the London area. These locomotives, which actually belonged to the '4575' class, were a Collett development of Churchward's '45xx' class for light branch-line work, the main external difference being the fitting of larger water tanks with a sloping top (compared with the flat-topped type carried by the earlier locomotives). *Author*

Above: Pannier tanks of various types were the mainstay of empty-stock workings into and out of Paddington during the steam era. Seen at Old Oak Common carriage sidings in December 1964 is one of Hawksworth's weighty examples, No 9415. The author's first footplate ride was on sister engine No 9410 along the length of one of Paddington's platforms — a great thrill for a small boy who had merely asked to climb on the footplate. *Author*

Right: Yarnton, west of Oxford, was the junction for the Fairford branch and boasted an unusual cast-iron urinal on one platform. Heavy-freight 2-8-0 No 3863 was visiting on 15 August 1965, having taken charge of a railtour at Reading, for which it had been specially cleaned. As proclaimed on the buffer-beam, the engine hails from Bristol. *Author*

Left: Standing outside the engine shed at Aylesbury, the photographer has captured another auto-fitted pannier tank, this time a member of the '64xx' class — similar in appearance to the '54xx' class (as featured on page 10) but with smaller wheels. The locomotive has been painted in lined green, but this is only visible on the cab side and bunker. The train has arrived from Princes Risborough, with the engine attached to a compartment trailer rather than the traditional saloon trailer. *Charles Firminger*

Above: Although Reading might not have seemed an obvious home for the 'Castle' class, there were always a few shedded there and, judging from this photograph, they were well-groomed. No 5018 *St Mawes Castle* catches the evening sunlight as it stands in front of a '2251' 0-6-0 light mixed-traffic engine, which was more typical of Reading's locomotive stud. *Charles Firminger*

The main steam shed at Old Oak Common was built in 1906 and was a huge structure comprising what were, in effect, four roundhouses under a single roof. This view dating from April 1963 shows two presentable locomotives standing around one of the turntables —

No 6921 *Borwick Hall* and No 5076 *Gladiator*. The latter is, of course, a 'Castle', its name referring not to a Roman fighter but to the Gloucester biplane, three of which defended Malta unaided in the autumn of 1940. *Geoff Rixon*

The 6.25am Penzance–Paddington express passes through Sonning Cutting in the summer of 1959, hauled by No 1019 *County of Merioneth*. Hawksworth's 30 'Counties' were powerful mixed-traffic engines, larger than the 'Halls' in terms of driving-wheel diameter and size of boiler (the latter being based on that carried by the Stanier '8Fs' built at Swindon during World War 2). However, until fitted with double chimneys they were generally indifferent performers, and by the time the whole class had been modified time was running out for steam traction. All were withdrawn between 1962 and 1964, after less than 20 years' service. *Ken Wightman*

Left: Slough was the junction for the short branch to Windsor & Eton and also boasted a small engine shed. Large Prairie tank No 6160 was photographed standing on the coaling stage road in May 1962. In the background is the site of Slough's new signalbox; part of the old 'box can be glimpsed behind the engine. *Geoff Rixon*

Above: A rare bird takes the east curve past Didcot engine shed in May 1963, hauling a train of empty coal wagons. The locomotive is 2-8-2 tank No 7218 from Oxley shed (84B) and was withdrawn two months later. The '72xx' class comprised 54 former 2-8-0 tanks rebuilt with extended framing to allow for a trailing axle, enlarged water tanks and a huge bunker, thereby extending their range of operation. *Geoff Rixon*

Above: Heading for Birmingham a few weeks before 'dieselisation' of these services from London, No 6001 *King Edward VII* passes under Bishop's Bridge Road on 6 July 1962. This unusual perspective of a Paddington departure was achieved by the photographer's leaning out of the window of an incoming local train. *Geoff Rixon*

Right: The GWR's 'greyhounds' at the beginning of the 20th century (before the 'Saint' class went into production) were the 'City' 4-4-0s, of which No 3440 *City of Truro* is widely regarded as having been the first steam locomotive to exceed 100mph. Withdrawn from service in 1931 to become a museum exhibit, the locomotive was put back into service in 1957 for four years. This view shows it passing Wormwood Scrubs on 18 August 1957 at the head of an incredibly long special train to Swindon, with Old Oak Common sheds in the background. *Ken Wightman*

Above: Against the backdrop of High Wycombe's distinctive retaining wall, large Prairie tank No 6111 approaches the station in September 1965 with a freight train from the Princes Risborough direction. After taking water, the train proceeded down the Bourne End/Maidenhead line. *Author*

Right: The Churchward Moguls were rugged little engines which could be entrusted with demanding work, not least when No 5380 was called upon to haul the up 'Bristolian' on 9 June 1960 following a diesel failure. In this view, recorded on 8 September 1962, the same engine has been given another formidable task as it heads a down express through Tilehurst. Unfortunately it sustained a badly bent running-plate and buffer-beam shortly afterwards and lay at Southall shed for some months before being towed away for scrapping. *Derek Penney*

Left: Jacob's Ladder, the nickname given to the footbridge to the west of West Ealing station (visible in the background), was a popular location for local trainspotters, including the author. This view from the bridge depicts pannier tank No 8752 shunting coal wagons in the down yard on 27 August 1962 and was the 14-year-old photographer's first colour picture. *Bill Piggott*

Above: No 7029 *Clun Castle* was the last of its celebrated class to remain in service and, even after official withdrawal by BR on 31 December 1965, continued to be used on occasional freight workings in the Birmingham area during 1966. By this time the locomotive was privately owned and based at Tyseley, where it still resides. On 3 April 1965 it was photographed crossing the River Loddon at Twyford, at the head of a special from Birmingham to Swindon via the Greenford loop. *Vernon Murphy*

Left: Exclusive to the London area were the 11 pannier tanks fitted with condensing apparatus to enable them to travel on the Underground (not the tube!) to reach the GWR's Smithfield goods depot, near Farringdon. In this view at Old Oak Common on 13 October 1963 the invisible crew, not content with replenishing No 9707's tanks, seem to be filling the bunker and cab with water as well! *Geoff Rixon*

Above: The branch from Watlington to Princes Risborough was closed to passengers on 1 July 1957 and the Watlington–Chinnor section to freight on 2 January 1961. This view of long-demolished Watlington station features a visiting railtour hauled by No 1473. The two intermediate stations (as distinct from the later low-level halts), at Aston Rowant and Chinnor, were built in 1872 in the same attractive style as Watlington, and a wonderful reconstruction of Chinnor station has been created by the Chinnor & Princes Risborough Railway, which operates part of the original line. *Charles Firminger*

Above: King Henry VIII (alias No 6013) is in full flight hauling the 7am from Weston-super-Mare to Paddington through Hanwell & Elthorne on 6 October 1958. Apart from the demolition of the down main-line platform (on the left of the picture), this station, dating from 1877, has been allowed to remain in a time-warp and is largely unchanged today. *Ken Wightman*

Right: When the Western Region introduced lined-green livery for all classes of locomotives liable to haul passenger trains, large Prairie tank No 6135 was one of the first engines to discard its coat of black. The locomotive is a treat to behold as it stands at Hayes & Harlington in May 1956 at the head of a local train to Paddington. *Jim Oatway*

Above: Brunel wanted his Great Western Railway from London to Bristol to be as straight and level as possible, which, combined with his broad gauge, would give passengers a fast and comfortable journey. Constructing Sonning Cutting to a maximum depth of 50ft was one of his major civil-engineering works, involving some 1,200 workmen and 200 horses (and no excavators). Entering the cutting from Reading in September 1961 is No 4928 *Gatacre Hall* on an up freight.
Derek Penney

Right: The last steam auto-train to Aylesbury stops at Monks Risborough & Whiteleaf Halt on its journey from High Wycombe on Sunday 17 June 1962. Motive power was Collett 0-4-2 tank No 1440, which had been decorated by the crew for the occasion. The author and a schoolfriend, wishing to return to Ealing Broadway, found themselves stranded at Aylesbury and begged a ride in the cab of the locomotive, which was travelling light-engine back to Princes Risborough. They were duly deposited just before the station, out of sight of officialdom! *Author*

Left: The 'Manor' 4-6-0s incorporated some parts from withdrawn Churchward Moguls, although only the first 20 of the class of 30 were actually built in GWR days. No 7818 *Granville Manor*, photographed in November 1963 at Reigate on a Banbury–Redhill freight, became a testbed in the early 1950s for various experiments to improve draughting. The result was successful, and the entire class so modified. *Roy Hobbs*

Above: The WR's last scheduled steam-hauled working: on 3 January 1966 No 6998 *Burton Agnes Hall* leaves Oxford with the 10.30am Bournemouth–York, which it hauled from Oxford to Banbury. Bought by the GWS a fortnight later for £2500, No 6998 steamed out of Oxford shed on 2 April 1966 to its new home at Totnes Quay in Devon and again moved, in steam, with No 1466, to Didcot on 2 December 1967. The locomotive returned to the main line on 1 October 1972. *Vernon Murphy*

Index of Locations

Front cover: BR Western Region succeeds magnificently in emulating the GWR by providing a spotless locomotive, No 5035 *Coity Castle*, and a rake of chocolate-and-cream coaches for the 'Torbay Express' — the 12 noon departure from Paddington to Kingswear. The train is seen approaching Hanwell & Elthorne on 6 October 1958. *Ken Wightman*

Back cover: The London area's final auto-train (push-pull) service was the affectionately nick-named 'Marlow Donkey', which outlived the Princes Risborough auto-trains by three weeks. This view, between Bourne End and Cookham, was recorded on the last day of steam, Sunday 8 July 1962, when No 1421 and its battered trailer, conveying the author and his mother, amongst others, plied between Marlow and Cookham (instead of Maidenhead, due to engineering works). *Roy Hobbs*

Full details of Ian Allan Publishing titles can be found on www.ianallanpublishing.com
or by writing for a free copy of our latest catalogue to: Marketing Dept., Ian Allan Publishing, Riverdene Business Park, Molesey Road, Hersham KT12 4RG.

For an unrivalled range of aviation, military, transport and maritime publications, visit our secure on-line bookshop at: www.ianallansuperstore.com

or visit the Ian Allan Bookshops in
Birmingham
47 Stephenson Street, B2 4DH; Tel: 0121 643 2496; *e-mail:* bcc@ianallanpublishing.co.uk
Cardiff
31 Royal Arcade, CF10 1AE; Tel: 02920 390615; *e-mail:* cardiff@ianallanpublishing.co.uk
London
45/46 Lower Marsh, Waterloo, SE1 7RG; Tel: 020 7401 2100; *e-mail:* waterloo@ianallanpublishing.co.uk
Manchester
5 Piccadilly Station Approach, M1 2GH; Tel: 0161 237 9840; *e-mail:* manchester@ianallanpublishing.co.uk
and (aviation and military titles only) at
The Aviation Experience, Birmingham International Airport
3rd Floor, Main Terminal, B26 3QJ; Tel: 0121 781 0921 *e-mail:* bia@ianallanpublishing.co.uk

or through mail order by writing to: Ian Allan Mail Order Dept., 4 Watling Drive, Hinckley LE10 3EY. Tel: 01455 254450.   Fax: 01455 233737. *e-mail:* midlandbooks@compuserve.com

You are only a visit away from over 1,000 publishers worldwide.